Go-To Guides

A **CAMPER'S GUIDE** to an
AWESOME
CAMPING TRIP

by Marne Ventura

CAPSTONE PRESS
a capstone imprint

Snap Books are published by Capstone Press,
1710 Roe Crest Drive, North Mankato, Minnesota 56003
www.mycapstone.com

Library of Congress Cataloging-in-Publication Data
Cataloging-in-Publication Data is available from the Library of Congress website.
ISBN: 978-1-5157-3662-2 (library binding)
ISBN: 978-1-5157-3665-3 (eBook PDF)
Summary: Activities, recipes, and games for camping

Editorial Credits
Jaclyn Jaycox and Abby Colich, editors; Juliette Peters, designer; Laura Manthe, production specialist;
Morgan Walters, media researcher; Sarah Schuette, photo stylist; Sarah Schuette and Marcy Morin,
project creators

Photo Credits
Capstone Studio: Karon Dubke, cover, (feet) 1, (chocolate) 4, (bug spray) 5, 16, 17, 7, 9, 10, 11, 13, 15, 19,
21, 22, 23, 24, 25, 27, 29; Shutterstock: Anna Shkolnaya, (tin foil) 26, AVN Photo Lab, (grill background)
6, bestv, (water bottle) 14, emodpk, bottom 30, endeavor, (crackers) 28, Freedom Man, (glow sticks) 8,
isak55, top right 31, bottom right 31, Maks Narodenko, (egg) 6, Maren Winter, (vanilla) bottom right 16,
mikolajn, 2, 3, oksana2010, (soap) 18, oneinchpunch, (people) bottom 4, pernsanitfoto, 20, Phil McDonald,
(duct tape) 14, rprongjai, (oven mit) 26, rukxstockphoto, (chocolate) 28, S_Photo, middle 5, SKY2015,
(night sky) 30, 31, Smit, (tree background) 5, Tadija Savic, (bubble background) 18, tsg.pictures, 32,
Tuangtong Soraprasert, (doll) bottom 24, varuna, (river) 1, videokvadrat, 12, Yuriy Kulik, left 31

Printed in Canada.
010040S17

TABLE OF CONTENTS

Camping Basics

If you love camping, you're not alone! More than 40 million Americans go on camping trips each year. There's something magical about sitting by a campfire and sleeping under the twinkling stars.

The recipes, crafts, and games in these pages will help turn a ho-hum camping trip into something awesome! Read through them before you go. Gather the supplies and materials you'll need. You'll be ready for some fun activities while taking in the sights, sounds, and smells of the great outdoors.

Before You Go

Whether you're new to camping or a camping pro, it's smart to be prepared. Learn about where you're going and bring the right gear.

Will it be hot or cold?
Will you be swimming or hiking?
How will you be cooking your food?
Where will you sleep?

The trick is to bring as little as possible, but still have everything you need.

TIP: Remember, good campers take care of themselves and their campsite. Read the signs and follow safety rules. Respect the plants, animals, and other campers around you. Take home everything you bring in. Leave your area cleaner than you found it. Let adults handle the campfire. Most of all, have fun!

Brown Paper Eggs

Who knew you could make bacon and eggs without a skillet? Use a brown paper bag for a pan and serving dish instead. It also makes for super easy cleanup!

You will need:
- campfire or barbeque
- paper bag
- butter or cooking spray
- 1 slice Canadian bacon
- 1 egg
- long tongs
- oven mitt or pot holder
- 1 slice of cheese
- paper plate
- seasonings (optional)

Step 1
Ask an adult to get a barbeque or campfire ready. You will need a grill over medium heat or hot coals (no flame).

Step 2
Coat the inside bottom and lower sides of the paper bag with butter or cooking spray.

Step 3
Place the Canadian bacon on the bottom of the bag. Break the egg and pour it onto the bacon. If you like the yolk soft, leave it unbroken. If not, poke the yolk and stir it around a bit. Fold the top of the bag down two or three times to close.

Who Invented Camping?

Before the late 1800s, camping was not something people did for fun. Early American settlers camped because there were few hotels or inns along the way. Why did people start camping by choice? A man named Thomas Hiram Holding started the camping-for-fun craze when he published *The Camper's Handbook* in 1908.

Step 4

Use tongs and an oven mitt to place the bag on the grill.

Step 5

After about ten minutes, use an oven mitt and tongs to take the bag off of the grill. Open the bag carefully and drop in a slice of cheese. Close the bag and return it to the grill for a minute to melt the cheese.

Step 6

Remove the bag from the grill. Place it on a paper plate. Tear away the sides of the bag to make a bowl. Season as desired.

TIP: To complete your meal, pack muffins and aluminum foil. Five minutes before the bacon and eggs are done, place a foil-wrapped muffin on the grill. Or toast a split English muffin on the grill during the last five minutes and make a sandwich. Don't forget some fresh fruit!

Glow Stick Tic-Tac-Toe

Glow sticks are useful for more than you might think. Not only are they pretty and easy to bend into different shapes, they can make a simple game extra fun!

You will need:
- 8 red glow sticks
- glow stick connectors
- 5 green glow sticks
- 5 blue glow sticks

Step 1

After dark, find a clear, flat area such as the ground or a picnic table.

Step 2

Connect the red glow sticks to make four long sticks. Lay them on the ground or table to form a tic-tac-toe grid.

Step 3

Use connectors to form circles with the green and blue glow sticks. Player one uses green circles. Player two uses blue circles. (Any three colors will work for the grid and player's pieces.)

Step 4

Two players start. The winner plays a second game against a new player. Continue until everyone has played. Keep score to see who gets the most wins. The winner gets the first s'more!

Glow Stick Ring Toss

Make rings by connecting two glow sticks into a circle. Set a bottle on a table or the ground. Take turns seeing how many rings you can land on the bottle.

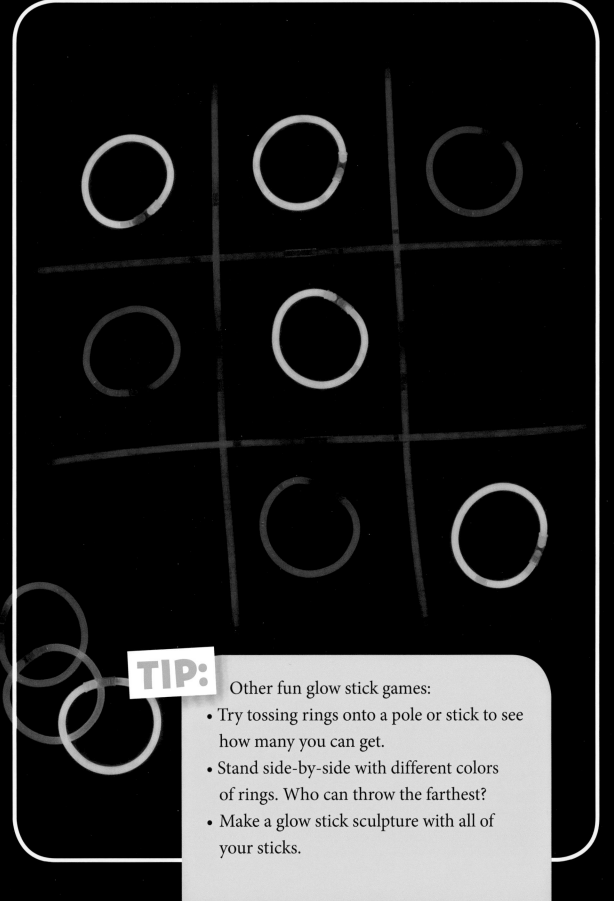

9

TIP: Other fun glow stick games:
- Try tossing rings onto a pole or stick to see how many you can get.
- Stand side-by-side with different colors of rings. Who can throw the farthest?
- Make a glow stick sculpture with all of your sticks.

Camper's Solar Cooker

Want a hot lunch without lighting the campfire? Solar cooker to the rescue! This clever contraption turns a pizza box into an oven by using energy from the sun. Who knew lunch in the wild could taste so good?

You will need:
- clean pizza box with lid
- black construction paper
- newspaper
- clear tape
- ruler
- box cutter
- aluminum foil
- plastic wrap
- stick or ruler

Step 1

Cover the inside bottom of the pizza box with black paper. Roll the newspaper sheets and tape them around the edges inside the box.

Step 2

Close the box. Measure and mark a 1-inch (2.5-cm) border on the front, left, and right sides of the box top. Ask an adult to cut along the marks to make a flap. Fold the flap up.

Step 3

Cover the inside of the flap with foil. The shiny side should face out.

Step 4

Tape two sheets of plastic wrap over the hole in the lid on the inside. Seal the hole completely.

High Noon Pizza

Top mini pita breads with tomato sauce and shredded mozzarella cheese. Heat four at a time in a solar cooker until the cheese is melted.

Step 5

Around noon, when the sun is hottest, open the box and place food inside at the center. Close the lid tightly and use a stick or ruler to prop the flap so it reflects sunlight onto the food.

Step 6

When the food is ready, remove carefully.

Scavenger Hunt

You need to be careful not to harm or disturb plants, rocks, and animals in nature. But you can still have a fun scavenger hunt! Check off the items on your list instead of collecting them. Put the lists together before you leave home.

You will need:
- checklists of items to search for
- scissors
- 4- x 6-inch (10- x 15-cm) sheets of craft foam
- glue stick
- hole punch
- ribbon or twine
- markers (or pens)
- clear tape
- whistle

Step 1
Trim the checklists to fit on the craft foam.

Step 2
For every two campers, glue a checklist to the front of a sheet of craft foam.

Step 3
Punch a hole in one corner of the craft foam. Cut a 3-foot (0.9-m) length of ribbon or twine. Tie one end in the hole.

Step 4
Tie the other end of the ribbon around the marker. If needed, add a piece of clear tape to secure the ribbon to the marker.

Nature Lover's Scavenger Hunt

- triangle-shaped rock
- something fuzzy
- something noisy
- 3 types of leaves
- a seed
- 3 things that fly
- a flower with 5 petals
- an insect
- a spider
- a feather
- a cloud shaped like an animal

Step 5

To play, pick a hiking area and hunt in teams of two. Players check items off the list as they find them.

Step 6

At the end of 30 minutes, blow a whistle to tell campers to come back to the starting point. The team with the most items checked wins.

Scavenger Hunt
☐ Heart-shaped leaf
☐ Flat rock
☐ Pinecone
☐ Dandelion
☐ Lizard
☐ Fallen flower petal
☐ Something red
☐ Wood chip
☐ Feather
☐ Acorn
☐ Berry

Be sure to stay on marked trails while doing your scavenger hunt!

TIP: If you have enough digital cameras or smartphones, take photos of the items on the list as you find them.

Camper's Water Caddy

Smart campers stay hydrated with clean drinking water. But who wants to carry a bottle? Keep your hands free with this fun, easy project. It's waterproof and washable, so feel free to get wet and dirty!

You will need:
- measuring tape
- insulated drink holder
- duct tape in two colors
- scissors
- water bottle

Step 1
Use measuring tape to measure the distance around the drink holder. Add 2 inches (5 cm).

Step 2
Cut a piece of duct tape the length of your measurement. Wrap it around the top of the drink holder, overlapping the edge.

Step 3
Continue to cut and wrap lengths of duct tape around the drink holder until it is completely covered. Leave the bottom uncovered.

Step 4
Use the measuring tape to decide how long you want your shoulder strap. Cut a length of duct tape this long plus 2 inches (5 cm). Ask a friend to help you fold it in half lengthwise.

Step 5
Use one more length of duct tape to attach the shoulder strap.

Step 6
Add a stripe of contrasting duct tape to the center of the holder to match the shoulder strap.

TIP: Sometimes insulated drink holders come free with drinks. If you can't find one around the house, try a dollar store.

Homemade Insect Repellent

Don't let bug bites distract you from all the fun you'll be having on your camping trip. Make this homemade repellent before you leave. Spray on as needed. Homemade bug repellents are effective, and they smell good too. Lemon eucalyptus oil helps keep mosquitoes at bay. The vanilla helps keep the mixture from evaporating off your skin too quickly.

You will need:
- 8-ounce (236-mL) spray bottle
- witch hazel
- funnel (optional)
- 1 teaspoon (5 mL) real vanilla extract (not artificially flavored)
- lemon eucalyptus oil
- eyedropper
- filtered water

Step 3
Fill the rest of the bottle with filtered water. Shake to mix the ingredients.

Step 4
Spray on exposed skin before going outside. Be sure it does not get into your eyes, nose, or mouth. Do not use on any open scrapes or cuts. Reapply every few hours. Shake well before each use.

Step 1
Fill the spray bottle halfway with witch hazel. Use the funnel if your spray bottle has a narrow opening.

Step 2
Add the vanilla and about 30 drops of the lemon eucalyptus oil into the bottle.

TIP: The Centers for Disease Control and Prevention (CDC) says that lemon eucalyptus oil is safe and effective in helping to prevent mosquito bites. If you're going to an area where ticks are prevalent, visit the CDC website for a list of safe and effective natural oils that help keep ticks away. Try making a spray using those oils.

17

Soap Pouch

Showering at your campsite will be so much easier with this soap pouch. Make it before your trip, and when it's time to shower, just grab and go.

You will need:
- washcloth
- ruler
- scissors
- sewing needle and thread
- 7-inch (18-cm) fabric ribbon
- bar of soap
- zip-top plastic bag

Step 1

Measure and cut the washcloth to about 4 x 10 inches (10 x 25 cm). At one of the shorter ends, fold the fabric up about 0.25 inches (0.6 cm) and sew to create a hem. Repeat for the other shorter end.

Step 2

Flip the fabric over. Take one shorter end and fold upward to about 2 inches (5 cm) below the other shorter end. Sew along each longer side. Then flip the pouch inside out.

Step 3

Fold ribbon in half. Sew ends of ribbon to inside of front edge of pouch. Use the ribbon as a carrying handle or hanger for your pouch. Stick the soap inside. Fold over and tuck in the top of the pouch to keep the soap inside.

Step 4

Store your soap pouch in a zip-top plastic bag. This will keep it clean beforehand and prevent it from getting your things wet after use.

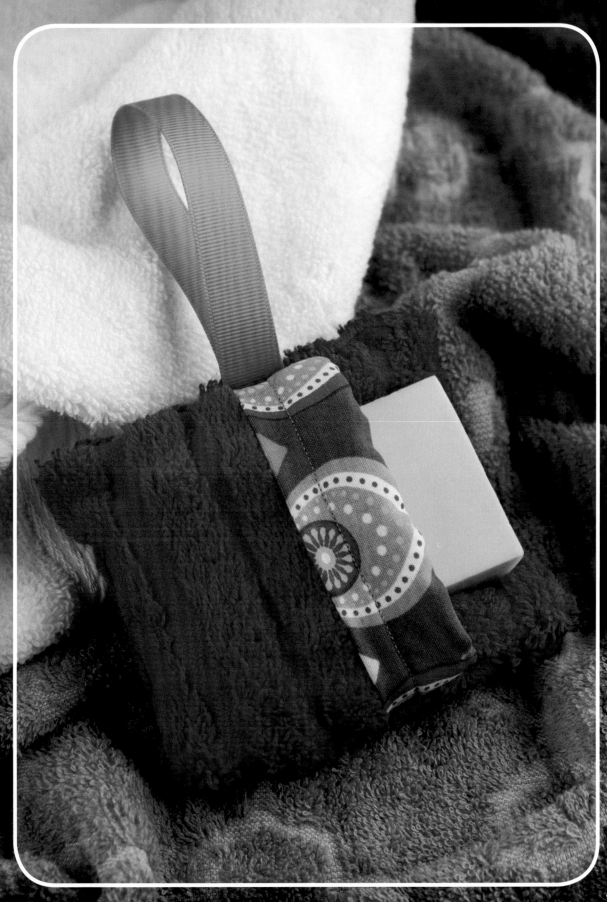

Butterfly Leaf Art

Gather some pretty fallen leaves and transform them into art! The more different shapes and colors of leaves you can find, the better.

You will need:
- a paper bag for collecting leaves
- scissors
- white glue
- white or buff cardstock
- ruler
- pencil, pen, or marker
- a sheet of colored cardboard or cardstock
- nature-related rubber stamps and ink pad

Step 1
Go for a walk and collect leaves from the ground. Get a variety of sizes, shapes, and colors. Remember to only take leaves that are not attached to a living plant.

Step 2
Back at camp, arrange the leaves in a butterfly shape. Use small leaves as is. Cut out the parts of a butterfly including two wings, antennae, and the thorax from big leaves.

Step 3
Once you're happy with your design, glue the leaves in place on the cardstock. If the leaf is curling, flip it over so the part that sticks out is glued. Dry completely.

Step 4
Measure, mark, and trim the edges of the white cardstock to make a square extending about 1.5 inches (3.8 cm) beyond the butterfly.

Step 5
Trace around the white cardstock square in the middle of a sheet of colored cardstock. Measure and cut 1 inch (2.5 cm) out from the edges to make a frame. Glue the white cardstock onto the colored cardstock frame.

Step 6
Decorate the frame of your artwork using your rubber stamps. You could also dip leaves in the ink to make a leaf stamp.

Step 7
Don't forget to sign your art!

TIP: Instead of framing your butterfly, glue it to the cover of a journal. Write about your camping trip inside.

Branch Weaving

What's one of the best things about camping? Arts and crafts! With no school, homework, chores, or practice, you've got free time. Find a Y-shaped branch and settle in for a weaving project. When you're done, you'll have an awesome souvenir or gift.

You will need:
- a Y-shaped twig, about 7 inches (18 cm) at the widest part
- sandpaper
- cotton twine
- scissors
- four or more colors of thick yarn
- needle with large eye

Step 1
Ask an adult to help you trim or sand any sharp places on your Y-shaped twig.

Step 2
Tie the end of the ball of cotton twine around one of the Y branches near the fork. Wrap it around the branch and then pull it across to the other side. Wrap it around and pull it back across to the bottom of the opposite side. Repeat, moving up the Y until it's strung to the widest part. Tie off the end and cut.

Step 3
Cut a 20-inch (50-cm) length of colored yarn and thread it through the eye of the needle. Starting at one inner side of the wide end, weave the colored yarn in and out.

Step 4
At the end of two or three rows, take the needle off of the yarn and let the end hang toward the back.

Step 5
Thread a new 20-inch (50-cm) length of a different color of yarn. Weave the yarn in and out for two or three rows.

Step 6
Continue weaving until the Y is full. Let the ends hang out the back side. For wider stripes, use a longer piece of colored yarn and weave more rows.

Step 7
Trim, tie off, or glue the ends on the back side of the weaving.

TIP: The tighter you can get your weaving, the better it will look. Use a fork to push back the rows as you weave.

Fairy House Garden

What do you like best about fairies? They're tiny, imaginary, magical, human-like, and they can fly. Build a little house with a beautiful garden at the base of a big tree for the forest fairies. Take a walk and search for materials on the ground—the smaller, the better!

You will need:
- bag or box for materials
- sticks and twigs
- pieces of bark
- stones
- moss
- pinecones
- flowers and petals
- leaves
- acorns
- nuts and nut shells
- seashells
- empty snail shells
- seeds
- seedpods
- pine needles
- dry grass

Step 1
Take a bag or box and go on a nature walk to gather materials.

Step 2
Pick a building site at the base of a tree. Flat ground or an opening in the trunk work well.

Step 3
Stick four twigs into the ground for the corners of the house. Use flat sections of bark to form the side and back walls of the house. Or use side-by-side twigs like logs.

Step 4
Lay flat bark pieces or twigs over the top to form a roof. A bit of mud will help stick pieces together if needed.

Step 5
Use stones to line a walkway up to the house.

Step 6

Make a rug for the front door or inside of the house with moss. Or cut a leaf into a rug shape.

Step 7

Use your materials and your imagination to come up with more decorations and furnishings. The cap of an acorn makes a good planter or bowl. Stones or bark can be tables and chairs. Pinecones are good for trees, and twigs can make a fence.

TIP: Don't touch poison oak or poison ivy! If you do, you'll get a red, itchy rash. Poison ivy grows as a vine or bush. It has green pointed leaves that hang from the stem in groups of three. Poison oak leaves also hang in groups of three but they have ruffled edges.

Foil-Wrapped Meal

What is it about camping that makes everyone so hungry? This dinner is quick and easy to prepare. With your own packet, you can put whatever you like in it. You can eat right out of the foil packet. Cleanup is easy!

You will need:
- barbeque or grill set over a campfire
- aluminum foil
- cooking spray
- 1 pound (450 g) fully cooked chicken or other meat
- knife
- 6 medium red-skinned potatoes
- 36 baby carrots
- barbeque sauce
- oven mitt or pot holder
- paper plates

Step 1
Ask an adult to prepare a grill over a medium-heat barbeque or campfire with hot coals.

Step 2
Tear off six squares of aluminum foil. Spray each one with cooking spray.

Step 3
Cut the meat into 1-inch (2.5 cm) pieces. Divide evenly between the foil sheets.

Step 4
Wash the potatoes and cut into 1-inch (2.5-cm) chunks. Divide evenly between the foil packets.

Step 5
Add six baby carrots to each packet.

Step 6
Drizzle each packet with barbeque sauce.

Step 7

Fold up two sides of the foil squares and seal well. Seal the other two sides.

Step 8

Place packets on the grill and cook for 20 to 30 minutes.

Remove one packet with oven mitts and place on a paper plate. Open carefully, watching out for steam. Poke a potato and carrot with a fork. If they feel soft, it's done. If not, seal it up and cook another 5 to 10 minutes.

TIP: The possibilities for foil packet dinners are endless! Try prebaked meatballs, precooked pasta, mushrooms, and marinara. Or how about cooked chicken chunks, precooked rice, stir-fry veggies, and teriyaki sauce?

27

S'Mores Dipping Boats

Here's a fun twist on s'mores, the traditional camper's dessert. Melt chocolate, marshmallows, and peanut butter in a banana. Then scoop up the goodness with graham crackers.

You will need:
- aluminum foil
- banana
- sharp knife
- butter knife
- peanut butter
- mini chocolate chips
- mini marshmallows
- graham crackers
- oven mitt or pot holder
- paper plates

Step 1
For each banana, tear off a square of foil. Place a banana on each square.

Step 2
Have an adult make a lengthwise slice through the banana. Do not cut through to the bottom. Press the ends of the banana gently to open the slit.

Step 3
Spread the inside of the slit banana with peanut butter.

Step 4
Fill the opening of the banana with chocolate chips and mini marshmallows.

Step 5
Wrap the foil around the banana. Make sure it's sealed.

Step 6
Place the foil-wrapped banana on a grill over medium heat or burning coals.

Step 7
After about ten minutes, use an oven mitt or pot holder to move the foil-wrapped banana to a couple of paper plates. Open carefully, watching out for steam.

Step 8
Scoop up your banana boat dip with graham crackers. Yum!

TIP: Spread the inside of a sugar cone with peanut butter and fill with chopped banana, mini chocolate chips, and mini marshmallows. Wrap in foil and grill for ten minutes. Remove with an oven mitt, unwrap carefully, and enjoy!

Campfire Games

People have gathered around a fire at night for thousands of years. It's a special time to be together, tell stories, play games, sing songs, and enjoy the night sky. Here are just a few ideas to get you started.

Fact or Fiction

Each camper tells three "facts" about him- or herself. Two are true. One is false. The other campers take turns guessing which "fact" is actually fiction. After everyone has guessed, the camper reveals the answer.

Spooky Story Circle

One camper starts a spooky story with a sentence such as, "It was a dark and stormy night." The camper to her right continues the story by adding a sentence such as "Ashley was home alone." The camper to her right adds a sentence, and so on. Keep going until everyone has had a turn or the story comes to an end.

Flashlight Tag

For an active break from sitting around the campfire, move to a dark but safe open area. One camper has a flashlight. The others have to run out of the path of the light. If the light from the flashlight hits a person, she is out and has to go back to the campfire. The last one out is the winner and gets to shine the flashlight for the next round.

Stargazing

One of the best parts of camping is looking up at the night sky and seeing all the beautiful stars. While you are admiring the view, see if you can spot any of these constellations:

Orion

Orion is the largest and one of the most visible constellations. It can be seen all over the world.

Ursa Major

The Big Dipper is part of the Ursa Major constellation.

Ursa Minor

The Little Dipper is part of the Ursa Minor constellation.

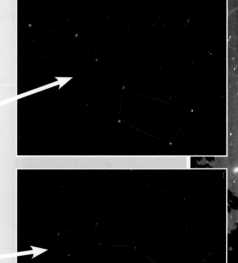

TIP: Look for meteor showers during the summer months. July and August are two of the best months to see shooting stars.

Read More

Butterfield, Moira. *Survive and Thrive: A Pocket Guide to Wilderness Safety Skills.* Hauppauge, N.Y.: Barron's Educational Series, 2016.

Hamilton, Linda Parker. *Camping Activity Book for Families: The Kid-Tested Guide to Fun in the Outdoors.* Guilford, Conn.: FalconGuides, 2016.

Howard, Melanie A. *Camping for Kids.* Into the Great Outdoors. Mankato, Minn.: Capstone, 2013.

Tornio, Stacy, and Ken Keffer. *The Kids' Outdoor Adventure Book: 448 Great Things to Do in Nature Before You Grow Up.* Guilford, Conn.: FalconGuides, 2013.

Internet Sites

FactHound offers a safe, fun way to find Internet sites related to this book. All of the sites on FactHound have been researched by our staff.

Here's all you do:

Visit *www.facthound.com*

Type in this code: 9781515736622

Super-cool stuff! Check out projects, games and lots more at **www.capstonekids.com**